Cover Art "O'Battle" by Suzy Snow

# HEROES

## GREAT CHARACTERS OF THE BIBLE

## Steaven R. Snow

*LinAven Publications*

# Table of Contents

Lesson 1—*Adam* ..................8
Lesson 2—*Enoch* ................10
Lesson 3—*Noah* .................13
Lesson 4—*Abraham* ..............16
Lesson 5—*Sarai, Sarah* .........19
Lesson 6—*Joseph* ...............22
Lesson 7—*Moses* ................25
Lesson 8—*Rahab* ................28
Lesson 9—*Gideon* ...............31
Lesson 10—*Deborah & Barak* .....34
Lesson 11—*Samson* ..............37
Lesson 12—*Jephthah* ............40
Lesson 13—*David* ...............43
Lesson 14—*Samuel* ..............47
Lesson 15—*Nathan* ..............50
Lesson 16—*Elijah* ..............53
Lesson 17—*Elisha* ..............55
Lesson 18—*Isaiah* ..............58
Lesson 19—*Jeremiah* ............61
Lesson 20—*Ezekiel* .............64
Lesson 21—*Daniel* ..............67
Lesson 22—*Hananiah, Mishael, Azariah* ........70
Lesson 23—*Hosea* ...............73
Lesson 24—*Jonah* ...............76
Lesson 25—*Job* .................79
Lesson 26—*Esther* ..............82
Lesson 27—*Matthew* .............85
Lesson 28—*Peter* ...............88
Lesson 29—*James* ...............91
Lesson 30—*John* ................94

# Table of Contents

**Lesson 31—*John the Baptist*............................97**
**Lesson 32—*John Mark*.................................100**
**Lesson 33—*Luke*............................................103**
**Lesson 34—*Timothy*........................................106**
**Lesson 35—*Aquila & Priscilla*........................109**
**Lesson 36—*Apollos*........................................112**
**Lesson 37—*Onesimus*.....................................115**
**Lesson 38—*Thomas*........................................118**
**Lesson 39—*Philip, the Evangelist*..................121**
**Lesson 40—*Mary of Bethany*..........................124**
**Lesson 41—*Martha*.........................................127**
**Lesson 42—*Lydia*............................................130**
**Lesson 43—*Mary Magdalene*.........................133**
**Lesson 44—*Andrew*........................................136**
**Lesson 45—*The Woman at the Well*...............139**

*© 2009 by Steaven R. Snow*

*All rights reserved. No part of this book may be reproduced, stored in a retrieval system or transmitted in any form or by any means without the prior written permission of the publisher, except by a reviewer who may quote brief passages in a review to be printed in a newspaper, magazine or journal.*

*First Printing*

*LinAven Publications has allowed this work to remain exactly as the author intended, verbatim, without editorial input.*

**ISBN 10:** 1441466886
**ISBN 13:** 9781441466884

PUBLISHED BY LINAVEN PUBLICATIONS
www.publishedauthors.net/steavensnow

Printed in the U.S. by CreateSpace

# Great Characters of The Bible

### *Introduction*

*This series will introduce your class to both familiar and less familiar heroes of the faith. Please take nothing for granted with your students. Get to know them and teach them where they are. This series will enable you to relate to your class by introducing them to life lessons by meeting the heroes of the Bible.*

*This may mean in-depth teaching on familiar topics. Prepare yourself—your class will be able to tell. The minds of your students will grasp the teachings of God's Word by seeing it lived in the lives of real people...people who actually lived, facing real problems and learning real solutions.*

*May God richly bless you as you share these studies with your students.*

*Steaven R. Snow*

# LESSON 1

## Great Characters of The Bible

*Introduction: This lesson is designed to teach your class the importance of faith in and toward God and the failure of our works to please Him. It is the introduction of the Biblical example of the theme of a Blood Sacrifice as eventually fulfilled by Jesus Christ.*

### Abel

**Background Reading: Genesis 4:1-12 Text: Genesis 4:1-5; Hebrews 11:4; Key Verses Genesis 4:4-5**

Main Emphasis—the proper offering by faith

History—From the beginning of man outside the Garden of Eden, God has expected a sacrifice. It was required to be a blood sacrifice. Abel offered the sacrifice of a lamb, while his brother, Cain, offered a sacrifice of his labors—a gift of the harvest.

*Explain how this sacrifice points to Jesus, and how Cain's was the work of his own hands. This is an excellent opportunity to teach simply the deep truths of God's grace and man's works.*

Examples of visual aids:

1) Pictures of a lamb and a basket of vegetables or fruits
2) Picture of Jesus with verses in Scripture referring to Him as The Lamb
3) A scale with faith on one side and works on the other

*Use your imagination and come up with something with which you feel comfortable. Make it fit your age group!*

## Main Points

- **Faith alone saves, and not works**
- **Jesus is our sacrificial Lamb**

*NOTE: This lesson (as well as those that follow) can be adapted to many different age groups. It is recommended that as many age groups as possible teach the same lesson so that families will be able to discuss each particular week's study.*

# LESSON 2

## Great Characters of The Bible

*Introduction: This lesson is geared to teach your class the importance of pleasing God, and the far-reaching effects that can have—both in our present lives and our testimony to others who follow us later.*

### Enoch

**Background Reading: Genesis 5**
**Text: Genesis 5:21-25; Hebrews 11:5;**
**Key Verse Genesis 5:24**

Main Emphasis—pleasing God

History—Enoch was the great great great great grandson of Adam, and the father of Methuselah (the oldest person who ever lived.) Very little is given about Enoch; however, in Jude verse 14 he is quoted as a prophet, and in Luke 3:37, he is listed in the genealogy of Jesus Christ. He was part of the Ante-Deluvian Age (before the Flood), hence his advanced years.

*Explain that it is recorded in both passages that Enoch's legacy was that he pleased God, and God honored him by allowing him to not taste of death as a reward for his closeness to God.*

Examples of visual aids:

1) Two figures, walking toward a big house and away from a smaller one—get the children to understand that God simply invited Enoch to stay at His House—Heaven.
2) A shelf with two cans on it—label one can 'God' and the other can 'Self'. "Only 2 choices on the shelf—please your God or please yourself!"
3) A stamp pad, ink, and paper—use it to make thumb prints and show the class how they each make an individual mark for others to see later on.

*Use your imagination and come up with something with which you feel comfortable. Make it fit your age group!*

## Main Points

- **The importance of a close walk with God**

- **The importance of a good testimony**
- **God's rewards for faithfulness**

*Only two choices on the shelf; Please your God, or please yourself.*

# LESSON 3

## Great Characters of The Bible

*Introduction: This lesson is intended to give the student the opportunity to excel in witness before an evil audience. So many times, we yield to the ways of the world instead of standing up to be counted as being different. Noah was an example of the Christian walk by faith in a wicked generation—something we need today.*

### Noah

**Background Reading: Genesis 6:11-9:17**
**Text: Genesis 6:5-8, 22; Genesis 7:5; Hebrews 11:7; Key Verse Genesis 6:22**

Main Emphasis—doing God's will in the midst of ungodliness

History—The Ante-Deluvian civilization, of which Noah was a member, was a very wicked civilization. That civilization had reached the depths of depravity so low that

God's intention was to destroy the creature Man whom He had made, BUT "Noah found grace in the eyes of the LORD." While men's thoughts had turned to "evil continually," there was something about Noah that caused God to desire to rescue him—his faithful walk in the midst of evil.

*Explain how this lesson is important in our society today. Scripture says that Noah's days will be much like the days preceding Christ's return. As everything grows more and more wicked, it will be harder to stand for what is right—but it is still possible. Stress the importance of living a Godly life before an ungodly world.*

Examples of visual aids:
1) Pictures of Noah and the ark, animals, etc.
2) Candle, (or flashlight)—turn your lights out and show the effect of one small light in a roomful of darkness. Show your class that each of them can be a light in this world of darkness.

# Main Points

- **Obedience is doing what God says to do the first time He says to do it.**
- **Each of us can make a difference by being different.**

*<u>Stress to your class the importance of living a Godly life if they are Christians:</u>*
*1) We are not our own—we are bought with a price (Christ's Blood) I Cor. 6:20*
*2) It is our duty to live a godly life. Romans 6:12* <u>Don't be afraid to name sins!</u>

Obedience is our way of showing we believe God.

# LESSON 4

## Great Characters of The Bible

*Introduction: This lesson is intended to give the student a practical lesson in obedience to God. God often acts in ways that we do not understand, for His "ways are far above our ways." We sometimes stress obedience and followship only in areas that we understand. Sometimes we must trust God when we do not fully comprehend what is going on. Such is the case in this incident with Isaac.*

### Abraham

**Background Reading: Genesis 21-22**
**Text: Genesis 22:1-13; Hebrews 11:8-10;**
**Key Verses Genesis 22:7-12**

Main Emphasis—obeying even when we don't understand

History—Abraham had left the Ur of the Chaldees at God's command. Along the way he had seen the demise of Lot, the birth of Ishmael, and the barrenness of his wife Sarai (later Sarah). At the age of ninety-nine (Sarah being ninety), God granted them a miracle birth announcement and a baby was born named Isaac. He was the promise of God—through whom God would make a mighty nation of his descendants. By the time of this story, Isaac was a young man (probably in his mid to late teens), and God commanded Abraham to sacrifice him on Mount Moriah. The young man, Isaac, willingly carried all the makings for the sacrifice and willingly submitted himself to his father—even though he did not understand it. It was not until that dramatic end that God revealed His provision of a sacrifice.

*Explain how this lesson is a picture of the sacrificial substitute for our sins. Explain that the ram caught in the thicket was a symbol of our Substitute in Christ, and that Isaac's willingness to follow his father is a witness to us of how we should react in our Heavenly Father's Hand.*

Examples of visual aids:
1) Act out the story with the help of one of

your class members—older classes only
2) Cutout of a mountain. Label one side MORIAH. Label the other side CALVARY. Have a picture (or toy) of a ram and of a lamb. Explain how Jesus is that Lamb. (NOTE: it is believed that Moriah and Calvary <u>are</u> the same.)

**Main Points**
- **Faithfulness does not require understanding—just doing.**
- **God can be trusted—no matter what!**

*AS A LAMB LED TO THE SLAUGHTER*

# LESSON 5

## Great Characters of The Bible

*Introduction: This lesson is an excellent example of faith and obedience when common sense and reason "apparently" make more sense. All of us have faced the situation where not only does faith seem improbable, but it seems impossible as well. It is not always easy to believe in the face of overwhelming evidence, but it is still right to believe and act on that belief. Let us help our students see that "blind faith" (while that term is often derided) is sometimes the only faith we can have.*

### Sarai, Sarah

**Background Reading: Genesis 17-18**
**Text: Genesis 17:15-19; Genesis 18:1-15; Hebrews 11:11-12; Key Verse 18:14**

Main Emphasis—having faith when the situation seems to be impossible

History—Sarai had known the promise of

God to Abraham regarding a son. When it was apparent that she was past the age of child-bearing, she devised a plan whereby her servant, Hagar, would have a son to become the heir for Abraham. God had another plan. He fulfilled that plan to Abraham when he was a hundred years old and Sarai was ninety. God changed her name to Sarah (which means "noblewoman or princess"—Sarai meant "princess, but better 'my princess'".) What God was saying was that she was to be more than Abraham's wife—she was also to have the honor to be the "mother" of a great nation. When she heard it all for herself later, her first reaction was to laugh. God asked if there was anything too hard for the Lord.

*Explain how this lesson affects your class as individuals. Point out that it only takes one person to make a difference, and God uses people—one at a time to accomplish His will. Help your students see that each of them can be that one person.*

Examples of visual aids:
1) **Find a genealogy and point out how one life in the genealogy affects all of the others.**

2) Make a paper chain with your class. Label the chains with the names of your students. Show how each link is vital to the make-up of the chain. It makes a difference when one is missing. Individuals make a difference!

Main Points
- **Obedience in faith to the impossible is not foolishness; it is strength.**
- **Obedience in faith can change your life, as well as those around you.**

*PUT IT ON A PEDESTAL*

# LESSON 6

## Great Characters of The Bible

*Introduction: This lesson is an excellent example of doing right no matter what the circumstances. Many times, when everything seems to go wrong and we have done right, it is a great temptation to let our guard down. The temptation is to do as we please, because at times it seems that doing right has no positive reward. Such was the case with this young man Joseph. He was in a foreign land, sold into slavery—all because he had done right.*

### Joseph

**Background Reading: Genesis 37**
**Text: Genesis 39: 1-23, Key Verses 39: 21, 23**

Main Emphasis—doing right in the face of adversity

History—Joseph was seventeen years old when his brothers sold him into slavery because of their jealousy. His spirituality conflicted greatly with their worldliness, and they sold him into slavery to be rid of him. What seemed to be a waste was simply used by God to provide deliverance for His people. Joseph would rise to be comptroller over Potiphar's house (only to be done wrong again because of his righteousness.) From there he was thrown into prison and became an overseer, only to be let out to interpret the Pharaoh's dream and be made the Vice-Pharaoh of Egypt. It was in this capacity that he granted his brothers asylum during the great famine. Everything worked as God had planned because Joseph remained faithful.

*Explain how this lesson shows that obedience to God and faithfulness to Him is not contingent upon whether or not we are being treated fairly or justly. It is an opportunity to excel when the situation arises that may not reward the students 'adequately' for their actions.*

Examples of visual aids:
1) Use pictures of Joseph's Coat of Many Colors—stress its uniqueness.

2) Have two students do exactly the same small job. Reward one lavishly—give him a $5 bill; give the second a nickel. (It is right to do your best—no matter. . .)

**Main Points**

- **Faithfulness when the reward seems unfair for the actions**
- **Doing your best regardless of praise or reward**

*WHAT MAKES YOU WHO YOU ARE*

# LESSON 7

## Great Characters of The Bible

*Introduction: This lesson is intended to introduce your students to one of the greatest leaders in the Scriptures. Moses' life was not a perfect example of doing right at all times, but his qualities of leadership allowed God to use him as perhaps no other leader in the Old Testament was used. This lesson teaches us that God can and will use us if we simply submit to his authority and allow Him to work through us.*

## Moses

**Background Reading: Exodus chapters 2-4**
**Text: Exodus 3: 1-14, Key Verse 3: 11; Hebrews 11: 23-28**

Main Emphasis—learning who you are and how you fit into God's plan

History—Moses was born to Amram and

Jochebed during a time of great persecution. Pharaoh had given the command that all Jewish boy babies were to be slaughtered. Jochebed took her young son, placed him in an ark, and put him in the Nile River. Pharaoh's daughter discovered the baby and took him for her own—raising him in the Pharaoh's palace. After growing up and accepting responsibility as an Egyptian leader, he still struggled with his own identity as an Israelite. After murdering an Egyptian, he fled Egypt and wound up on the back side of the desert herding sheep. It was there that God chose to call him to deliver His people from bondage. Moses had to learn who he was so that God could use him.

*Explain how this lesson shows that each of us has his or her own potential, yet no one can reach that potential who does not know who he or she is and how he or she fits into God's plan for their lives. God does have a definite plan for our lives, which we call God's will. Success comes from knowing yourself and your God.*

Examples of visual aids:

1) A paper cut-out—on one side a kingly garb, the other something plainer.
2) Have your students write down on a piece of paper 2 columns—1) Who I Am 2) Who I Would Like to Be—Ask them to see how close reality is to desire.

**Main Points**
- **Knowing yourself and your place in God's will is essential for service.**
- **Accepting God's will for your life—even when you don't see it yourself.**

# LESSON 8

## Great Characters of The Bible

*Introduction: This lesson is intended to introduce your students to a great example of faith in the salvation of a family. This deliverance is an excellent example of how the burden of one can reach a group. With it, you will be able to show that a burden for the lost starts with just one person, and that God will honor the faith of just one person in seeking the salvation of others.*

### Rahab

**Background Reading: Joshua chapter 2**
**Text: Joshua 2: 5-15, Key Verses 2: 12 & 13; Hebrews 11: 31**

Main Emphasis—how one student can be used to see the salvation of others

History—Rahab was throughout the Scriptures known as Rahab, the harlot. Though her life was not what it should have been in the past, by faith she believed that the God of the Israelites was God. Because of hearing of the deeds in Egypt, she decided to put her trust in this God. When the spies came to search out Jericho, she hid them on the rooftop of her house. Because she lived on the wall of the city, she made possible their escape by letting them down the wall by a rope. Before the spies left, she made them promise to save her family from perishing in the upcoming invasion. The spies told her to tie a crimson sash from her window on the outside of the wall, and bring her family safely into the house. It worked!

*Explain how this lesson shows that each of us can have an active part in the salvation of those we love and care about. It was through her faith and her actions based upon that faith that her family was saved. Though we cannot have faith for those we love, we can earnestly seek to get them to a place where they can hear the Gospel or bring the Gospel to them.*

Examples of visual aids:
1) Acts 16: 31—written out with the word "house" emphasized.

2) Make a visible list of your students' lost loved ones—after making the list, ask "What would <u>you</u> be willing to do to see that person saved?" Make it personal!

## Main Points

- **While our faith cannot save others, it will lead to a burden of caring.**
- **The duty of every Christian is to do their best to win the lost.**

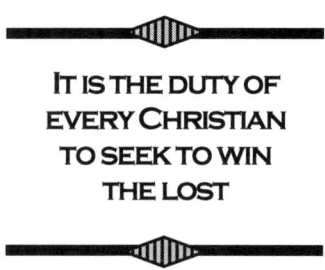

IT IS THE DUTY OF EVERY CHRISTIAN TO SEEK TO WIN THE LOST

# LESSON 9

## Great Characters of The Bible

*Introduction: This lesson is intended to help those students who feel that they are unimportant in God's sight. We often allow our social and economic status before men to determine what we think God can do <u>for</u> us, and <u>through</u> us. This story is the perfect example of one who did not come from wealth or fame who was used by God. It is an inspiration to those who might think that God cannot use them.*

## Gideon

**Background Reading: Judges chapters 6-8**
**Text: Judges 6:11-23, Key Verses 6: 15 & 16; Hebrews 11: 32**

Main Emphasis—to show that God can and does use the "nobodies"

History—As it was before the time of the kings of Israel, God used Judges to deliver

Israel at different times of need. When the Lord called Gideon to answer the call to be a Judge, it surprised Gideon. Gideon was from a small, 'unimportant' (or so he thought) family. God looked at him and saw things in his life that Gideon did not see in himself. When God looked at Gideon, He saw a "mighty man of valour." Gideon only saw himself as someone whom God could not use. What God did with Gideon proved that God wants to, and can, use anyone.

*Explain how this lesson shows that each of us is important in God's sight. It does not matter what is our family background or standing in the world's eyes. God looks to the heart of man and sees the qualities of character that make even those of us who feel we have nothing to offer, valuable. Stress how important it is to understand that God measures us differently than we do ourselves.*

Examples of visual aids:
1) A ruler and a cloth tape measurer—the ruler only measures distance, while the cloth tape can measure distance,

circumference, etc.—God's measuring vs. ours.
2) Paper labeled "Mighty Man of Valour" on one side; "The Least". Make a list from Judges 6-8 on each and compare them with your class—Both are Gideon.

**Main Points**
- **God wants to use each of us, no matter how little we think we are.**
- **The measurement of a man is the strength of his character—what it takes to stop him, even if that which stops him is himself.**

# LESSON 10

## Great Characters of The Bible

*Introduction: This lesson is intended to show that no matter what the odds are, God is never on the losing side. Sometimes we all tend to look at the Enemy rather than the Deliverer. It is during those times that we need the encouragement of those of like commitment as well as their comradarie. Such was the case in the lives of Deborah and Barak—two friends who, with God's help, served together.*

### Deborah and Barak

**Background Reading: Judges chapters 4-5**
**Text: Judges 4: 1-16, Key Verses 4: 15 & 16; Hebrews 11: 32**

Main Emphasis—to show that the battle and the victory are God's

History—Israel's history in the period of the Judges was a cyclical pattern—sin, judgment, and deliverance. Such was the case at this time. Israel had gone into sin and as a result had been delivered into the hands of the Canaanites. The leader of the Canaanite army was a general named Sisera. As a mighty warrior, he commanded a feared army of 900 chariots of iron. Israel was no match for this awesome power, but Deborah and Barak knew that God was.

*Explain how this lesson shows that no matter what the physical odds are, your outcome will be determined by your faith in God's ability to deliver. While we should never stress the "insurance" aspect of faith in God's ability, it is re-assuring to know that with God we are on the side of victory. Also explain how that sometimes it is easier to do God's will when we have someone with us. This is why unity in the church is so important. God promises to bless the strength that comes from unity.*

Examples of visual aids:
1) Bring a toy tank and a toy soldier. Place them in front of your students, and ask which is the more powerful. Relate it to

the lesson, and explain how God works.
2) 4 paper clips. Let 1 be God; let 1 be You; let 1 be Friend; and let the 4$^{th}$ be Power/Unity. Link You and Friend to God, with Power/Unity as the final link.

**Main Points**
- **God owns the victory, regardless of the battle.**
- **The outcome of the battle is often determined by our faith in God's ability to deliver.**
- **Unity allows us to experience victory.**

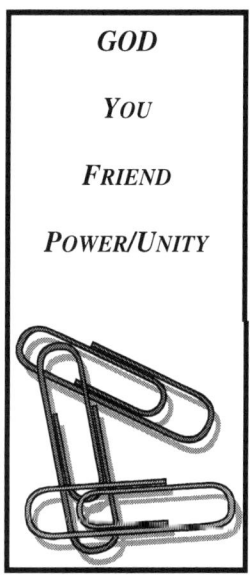

# LESSON 11

## Great Characters of The Bible

*Introduction: This lesson is intended to show that God's purpose can be performed in the life of someone who may not be as likely to be used by God as we might think. While God's desire is to use someone with as sterling a reputation as possible, sometimes He chooses a more unlikely candidate to do His will. Each of us has the potential to do God's will, even after we have failed.*

### Samson

**Background Reading: Judges chapters 13-16**
**Text: Judges 16: 20-30, Hebrews 11: 32; Key Verses 13: 24, 16: 21-22**

Main Emphasis—to show that God's grace is not negated by failure

History—Israel had once again, as in times before, returned to their sinning ways. A man by the name of Manoah had found grace in the eyes of the Lord, and he and his wife were granted a son who would be the deliverer of his people. An angel appeared to Manoah's wife and instructed her to not give her child strong drink or unclean foods, and to have him take the vow of the Nazarite—no razor ever to touch his head. God was preparing a child to be a clean vessel for His glory, but Samson was the epitome of a failure in many areas.

*Explain how this lesson shows that while God has a perfect plan for our lives, it is left up to each of us to do what He wishes. It is often through our failures that we learn the biggest lessons. This is not meant to excuse sin or unholy living, but is meant to show us that God's mercy is never failing. If we could merit or earn mercy, then it would cease to be mercy. Mercy is imparted to those who deserve it the least. Samson's life is not an endorsement <u>to</u> sin, but rather an encouragement to the <u>sinner</u>—God still forgives and wants to use us, even if at first we fail Him.*

**Examples of visual aids:**
1) Bring a dirty glass and a clean one—both can still hold water, but ask your class which one they would choose to drink from. Would they throw it away or clean it?
2) On a chalkboard or white board make a heavy line. Wipe it away. . .some still remains. The marks of sin perhaps will fade, but close inspection reveals them.

## Main Points
- **God wants to use each of us as clean vessels.**
- **God will not throw us away when our vessel gets dirty—his mercy is real.**

*THOUGH THE PENALTY OF SIN IS FORGIVEN,*

*OFTEN THE MARKS OF SIN REMAIN.*

# LESSON 12

## Great Characters of The Bible

*Introduction: This lesson deals with a most unusual man whom Scripture records as a great man of faith. It was Jephthah who made the vow of sacrifice for the first thing that walked through his doorway. That "thing" turned out to be his only child—his beloved daughter. As in all his dealings, he kept his word. Though he was not thought of highly for his beginnings (he was the son of a harlot), he was sought out for his abilities as a leader in Israel's time of need.*

## Jephthah

**Background Reading: Judges chapters 11-12**
**Text: Judges 11: 1-8, Hebrews 11: 32; Key Verses 11: 1, 11: 3**

Main Emphasis—to show that character can overcome experience

History—Gilead had a son, Jephthah, who was born of a harlot. When his wife had birthed two sons, those two sons as soon as they were able, forced Jephthah out of his father's home. Jephthah left and went to dwell in the land of Tob. As in the case of many young people who leave (for whatever reason) their parents' home, he became mixed up with the wrong crowd. God was not, however, through dealing with Jephthah. When trouble came, Jephthah was sought for his fighting skills. Jephthah, however, trusted God. His trust in God led to victory over the Amorites.

*Explain how this lesson shows that there really is no excuse of the wrong environment. Jephthah grew up with the stigma of not just being an illegitimate child, but the illegitimate child of a harlot. This could have stopped him from ever doing anything for God, but he chose not to blame God for his lot in life or his experiences. His choice was to follow God, and remain faithful to his God and faithful to his honor. He made that which was missing from his own life the strongest part of his character.*

**Examples of visual aids:**
1) Show 2 books with book covers. Beforehand, switch the book covers. Ask for the titles—don't judge a book by its cover!
2) Take a glass of water and take a drink. Put some dark food color in the water and drink again. Because you know the character (ingredients) you can still drink the water.

## Main Points
- **Environment does not necessarily determine character.**
- **God does not seek the perfect past, rather He seeks perfecting character.**

Don't judge a book by its cover, or a man by his past.

# LESSON 13

## Great Characters of The Bible

*Introduction: This lesson deals with the man whom Scripture refers to as "a man after God's own heart." Not only is he undoubtedly the greatest of all the kings of Israel, he was a man of God. This is not to say that he was perfect, but he humbled himself before his God, and kept a pure heart by keeping short accounts. If ever there was a man to learn from, it was David. His heart was tender (see the Psalms), yet he was a mighty warrior (remember Goliath.) Best of all, he was well rounded. He was just as much at home being godly as he was being manly.*

## David

**Background Reading: I Samuel 16-II Chronicles 35**
**Text: I Samuel 16:1-18, Hebrews 11: 32; Key Verses 16: 1, 7, 12, 17, 18**

Main Emphasis—God looks upon the heart

of man, not his outward appearance

History—Samuel had been mourning the apparent departure of God's power in the life of Saul. God told him to stop mourning and go find Jesse and anoint one of his sons as king of Israel. The stronger and older sons of Jesse were passed over by God, and he chose the young man, David, to have Samuel bless. While David may have looked like only a shepherd boy, God looked at him and saw a king. David's first place in the palace was that of a musician. It was he who calmed Saul down during his violently emotional mood swings.

*Explain how this lesson shows that while all men may look at your students and see only children or gangly teens or seemingly defeated adults, God looks at that which makes a person truly great—inner character. It is doing right when no one else is looking because doing the right thing is right. It is being willing to believe that God will do what He says He will do—when no one thinks He can. It has been said that "Greatness is not in the performance—it is in the preparation."*

Examples of visual aids:
1) Quiz Time! Ask "When William Tell shot the apple off his son's head with a bow and arrow, which was the greatest feat—that day or the practice for that day?" Emphasize <u>preparation</u>.
2) Find a picture of a person you admire when they were young. Show it to your class, and get them to guess what (not who) they are. Stress how hard it is to tell by just the <u>outside</u>.

## Main Points
- **True greatness reveals itself regardless of promotion.**
- **God is seeking to use someone whose heart is in tune with His.**

*PREPARATION*

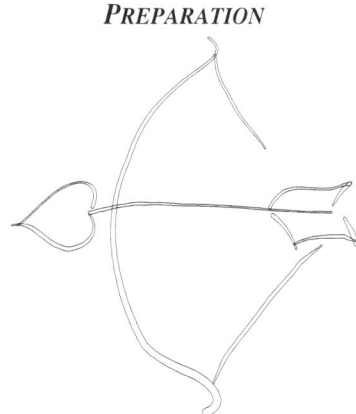

*THE KEY TO PERFORMANCE*

# LESSON 14

## Great Characters of The Bible

*Introduction: This lesson deals with a man who was used of God to show faithfulness in times of seeming rejection and who, after a life of service, seemed to be unappreciated. What is interesting and worthy of note is how he responded to this situation. As the purpose of these lessons is to show the events in different people's lives in developing or revealing character, it is here that we learn from Samuel that reward is not in recognition, but in responsibility.*

### Samuel

**Background Reading: I Samuel 12**
**Text: I Samuel 12:18-25, Hebrews 11:32; Key Verse 12:23**

Main Emphasis—to show that responsibility is key in the development of character

History—Samuel had been serving the

people faithfully for many years. The people had now come to him and requested that he anoint a king over them so that they could be like the other nations. Samuel had lived a holy life before the people from the time of his youth until now. He knew that God's will for the people was to have God as their King, and judges on earth. Now it seemed the people were rejecting not only God, but Samuel's ministry as well. His reaction is the focus of our lesson.

*Explain how this lesson shows that while events may unfold to reveal the lack of appreciation for your service, you will be faced with having to react to that situation. Samuel's heart was broken because of the people's sin of choosing a king; he held nothing against those who so chose, but rather urged them and warned them about walking with God afterward. Not only was his message still clear and plain, he knew that his responsibility was to continue to do as he had done before—pray for them, and teach them God's way and will.*

**Examples of visual aids:**
1) **Take two Pepsi bottles and draw the word Coke on one. Ask your class which of the two appears to be what it should be? Does**

that change the contents? Does a label change you?

2) Ask your class what is the difference between responsibility and duty. Make a list of the two, and then review that list with this in mind—Duty is that which you are obliged to do; responsibility is that which you agree that you <u>must</u> do.

## Main Points

- The strength of character is revealed in times of adversity.
- Responsibility and dependability are the greatest abilities.

Duty is that which you are obliged to do; responsibility is that which you agree that you must do.

# LESSON 15

## Great Characters of The Bible

*Introduction: This lesson deals with a man who was used of God to show that sometimes, even though the task at hand may seem difficult, it is still right to bear God's witness to those who need it. Nathan was the prophet that God chose to tell the mighty King David that God was going to judge him for his sin. Confrontation may not be the most welcome of all social encounters, but it is sometimes needed. Nathan gives us the example of the man who trusted God and did not fear man.*

### Nathan

**Background Reading: II Samuel 12**
**Text:   I Samuel 12:1-15; Key Verses 12:1, 15**

Main Emphasis—to show that the messenger must remain true to the message

History—It is apparent from reading the

chapters prior to this one that Nathan was a well-respected friend of the king. It was Nathan who was chosen to tell King David that he could not build a temple for the Lord because he was a bloody man of battle. It was Nathan who was now standing before the king in open court and telling him face to face that he was a thief, an adulterer, and a murderer. He confronted David with his sin, and God used his boldness to humble David to the point of repentance

*Explain how this lesson shows that we may sometimes find ourselves facing those with whom we work, or with whom we play, or even our own families—facing the fact that we may be asked to stand in direct opposition to, and confronting a known sin in their lives. While it would seem to be much easier to simply ignore wrong, it is a far more nobler thing to stand for that which is right. We can make no difference in the lives of those we love if we accept their sin. When we stand and confront them, we are standing to help them.*

Examples of visual aids:
1) A mirror and Play Dough. Which reveals truth without conforming? Which conforms without regard to truth?
2) Make a list of things that you would stand for. Ask your class this question, "What do the things I will stand for reveal about (not me,) but about how I feel toward you?"

## Main Points
- **Truth is truth regardless of its direction.**
- **Confrontation of sin reveals love for the one confronted by the confronter.**

*REVEALING TRUTH*

# LESSON 16

## Great Characters of The Bible

*Introduction: This lesson deals with a man who was used of God to show each of us the power that a testimony of righteousness can provide. Often we feel that testimonies have to be "from the depths of sin" to be considered a 'good' testimony. Such is not the case, and it is apparent in this man, Elijah's, life. Here we have a powerful testimony based upon personal holiness and past example.*

### Elijah

**Background Reading: I Kings 17**
**Text: I Kings 17:17-24; Key Verses 17:18, 24**

Main Emphasis—Personal holiness is exemplified before man as God's Power.

History—The first sixteen verses of our Scripture selection deal with the story of the Widow of Zarephath. In it, we find

Elijah providing through her faith a cruse of oil and barrel of meal that did not fail during the whole time of the famine (three and one half years.) It was because of Ahab, king of Israel, and his sin that Elijah had prayed that it would not rain—and it did not! Elijah had gone where God said when the brook dried up, and that was to the widow's house. After this miracle of provision, her son fell ill and died. It is here we find Elijah doing God's will again.

*Explain how this lesson shows that we need to have a testimony like Elijah's. He was known for his faith, his powerful praying, his holy life, his obedience to the voice of God, and his ability to get things done from God. Not only was he well known for his good works, but his holy living was such that it convicted others of their shortcomings. Lest we find ourselves thinking that this is an unattainable goal, consider what Scripture says in James 5:17. We, too, can do God's will with His power.*

**Examples of visual aids:**
1) **A lamp with a three-way bulb. The more power, the more light! So it is with us and**

God. The more we yield ourselves to Him, the more power we have through Him.
2) A mirror with a back exposed. Turn the gray side up and ask your class to see themselves. Turn the mirror side toward them. Show that *it* hasn't changed—just its focus—in which direction it faces reveals its ability to serve best, and so it is with God.

## Main Points
- **Our lives should be seen by others to glorify God.**
- **Our level of power is determined completely by our level of yieldedness.**

*"Let your light so shine before men"*

# LESSON 17

## Great Characters of The Bible

*Introduction: This lesson deals with a man whose life exemplified faithfulness, loyalty and dedication. These are character traits that are sorely absent in the lives of most Christians today. What is amazing is that not only did he have these qualities, but he was not a person who flaunted his attributes before men. Amazingly his name never appears in the New Testament, yet he performed twice the miracles that Elijah did.*

### Elisha

**Background Reading: II Kings 2**
**Text: I Kings 2:1-15; Key Verses 2: 2-6, 9**

Main Emphasis—Loyalty is the foundational characteristic of leadership.

History—The call of Elisha is recorded in I Kings chapter 19. He was a man who was busy doing a work when God called him to work for Him. His devotion and loyalty to the man of God, his family, and to God Himself, was rightly set in order and recorded in God's Word as a tribute to his character. When he was a plowman, he was faithful. While he was a student at Elijah's side, he was faithful. From this displayed character quality, God was choosing a man who had proven himself already. The time was drawing near to the home-going of Elijah. Our lesson centers around the last hours of their time together.

*Explain how this lesson shows that faithfulness, loyalty and devotion are character qualities that one must develop as one goes through life. You don't grow up, get a diploma and become faithful. If you and I are not faithful over the little things, how can we expect to be trusted with the big things? The stress of this lesson should be to instill the character quality traits of loyalty and faithfulness now, not when we get into a position or "arrive" spiritually.*

**Examples of questions to ask your class:**
**1) How did Elisha show his loyalty to Elijah**

before the sons of the prophets?
2) How did Elisha's refusal to separate himself from Elijah prove his devotion?
3) What was the most important request Elisha made? Why do you thing he asked this?

## Main Points
- **Loyalty must be cultivated or it can never grow.**
- **Faithfulness before men is seen by God as a measure of faithfulness to Him.**

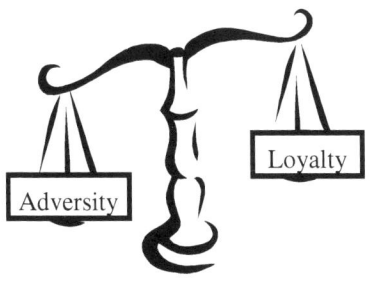

# LESSON 18

## Great Characters of The Bible

*Introduction: This lesson deals with a man whose vision of the holiness of God led to a personal holiness that was quite remarkable. Isaiah wrote much about the suffering Messiah. Isaiah 53 is remarkable in that it describes crucifixion perfectly—even though the Roman form of persecution had not been devised as yet. Through his encounter with the holiness of God in Isaiah 6, we find a man who exemplified holy living in his dealings with others. When King Hezekiah was later sick and dying, it was Isaiah that he called to pray.*

### Isaiah

**Background Reading: Isaiah chapter 6**
**Text: Isaiah 6: 1-10; Key Verses Isaiah 6: 5, 8**

Main Emphasis—Getting a vision of God will give you a vision for God.

History—Isaiah is one of the most interesting of all the prophets. He was privileged to receive a vision of the Lord "high and lifted up" and found himself to be "undone", "a man of unclean lips". Although the first appearance of Isaiah is with King Hezekiah in II Kings 19 in Scriptures, Isaiah chapter 6 occurs well before that recorded passage. Scripture chooses to introduce the man before his call. Uzziah was the first king under whose reign Isaiah would be prophet and chapter six of Isaiah records his call to the ministry.

*Explain how this lesson shows that there is a great need for us to understand that our God is a holy and righteous God. Far too often, we ascribe attributes to God that make Him more "manly," yet He describes His relationship to us as having thoughts "far above" our own. Too seldom, do we see the need for personal holiness in our own lives. When we get a correct view of the holiness of God, we shall seek to maintain our vision of God in reaching and ministering to others.*

**Examples of questions to ask your class:**
1) How did Isaiah see God? How do you see God? Can God be adequately defined?
2) What was Isaiah's response to his vision of God? What would you have done?
3) What was the outcome of this experience? How can you apply this to your life today?

## Main Points
- Holiness is an attribute which begets service.
- The measure of a man's holiness is his relationship to God.

# LESSON 19

## Great Characters of The Bible

*Introduction: This lesson is about a young man by the name of Jeremiah whom God called to be a prophet. Although he lived some seventy years after Isaiah, he was so well regarded that Jewish Scripture lists him first among the prophets. He was a very passionate man that wrote many times of the tears that he shed for his people. The Book of Lamentations was written by Jeremiah. This, along with the Book of Jeremiah, gives us the picture of a man who was not afraid to let his emotions be seen.*

### Jeremiah

**Background Reading: Jeremiah 1
Text: Jeremiah 1: 1-10; Key Verses Jeremiah 1: 5, 9**

Main Emphasis—God's will in our lives

History—Jeremiah's experience in his call to his prophetic office was somewhat similar to Isaiah's and Moses'. Isaiah made it known that he was "undone—a man of unclean lips"; Moses told God that he could not speak well; Jeremiah's excuse was that he was just a young man. God's choice for each of these men was exactly the correct choice for the situation at their time. God told Jeremiah that even before he was born, Jeremiah was chosen by God to do His will.

*Explain how this lesson shows that God has a definite plan for each of us. It may not be exactly as Jeremiah's, but He does have a plan that is as individual as we are. God chooses to call many young people because the hearts of young people are more receptive and their minds are more pliable to His training. Jeremiah would be persecuted, thrown in a dungeon, and eventually stoned to death for his acceptance of God's will in his life. We need to understand that the God of Heaven takes a personal interest in each of us to do His will as He leads us.*

**Examples of questions to ask your class:**
1) **Why do you think Jeremiah gave the excuse of being a child? How did God respond?**

2) How does this passage reflect on the sin of abortion in our time?
3) Jeremiah was called the Weeping Prophet. Was this a strength or a weakness?

## Main Points
- God has a definite will for each of us.
- There is no excuse that stands before God as good enough *not* to do His will.

# LESSON 20

## Great Characters of The Bible

*Introduction: This lesson is about a priest by the name of Ezekiel whom God called to do a work that could only be described as not being what Ezekiel would consider to be pleasant. God begins by telling him that He is sending him to a very rebellious people and that no matter what message he preached, they would not listen to him. Rather, they would choose to bind Ezekiel up and put him in prison. God had a plan in all of it—Ezekiel didn't understand and his attitude was evident in chapter three.*

## Ezekiel

**Background Reading: Ezekiel 1-5**
**Text: Ezekiel 3: 1-27; Key Verses: Ezekiel 3: 14-21**

Main Emphasis—What to do when we find God's will doesn't match our plans

History—Ezekiel, the priest, was the

prophet who had the visions of the wheel within a wheel and the valley of dry bones. He was a devout Jew who observed the Jewish law strictly. It was quite unpleasant when he discovered some of God's plans for his ministry. For example, while being struck dumb, he was to lay on his left side for 390 days, then 40 days on his right side, while drawing a picture of Jerusalem on a tile, using an iron skillet to portray the wall, and demonstrating a coming siege and the ensuing famine in mixing cow "patties" with barley, baking and eating them before the people.

*Explain how this lesson shows that God sometimes asks us to do some things that are unpleasant to us. This might be soul-winning (I can't talk to people; I'm too shy); it might be volunteering to do janitorial work (I don't do that at home!); it might be surrendering to a foreign field; or even surrendering to preach the Gospel. Often the work of God goes undone simply because we don't want to get our hands dirty. None of us have been asked to do what Ezekiel was asked to do.*

Examples of visual aids:
1) Bring an iron pot or skillet, a poster board (or something like that.) Demonstrate how Ezekiel had to lay on his side, unable to speak and yet testify.

## Main Points
- God has a definite will for each of us.
- If that will does not agree with our will, it is up to us to change...not God.

# *WHEN GOD USED A SKILLET*

# LESSON 21

## Great Characters of The Bible

*Introduction: This lesson is about a young man whose deep devotion allowed him to stand apart from others while holding true to his own beliefs and convictions. We often speak of and use the term "courage of our convictions" to define not only having convictions, but also being willing to stand for those beliefs as well. Daniel, though a teenager (in his later teens) at this time, chose to stand for what he believed when most others around him were choosing to conform.*

### Daniel

**Background Reading: Daniel 1:1-21
Text: Daniel 1: 1-8; Key Verse: Daniel 1:8**

Main Emphasis—Having the courage to stand for what we believe

History—Daniel was the son of a nobleman

in Israel, perhaps even one of the royal families. When Nebuchadnezzar captured Jerusalem in 606 B.C., the first who would be taken captive were the class of nobility—the ones capable of learning in the king's palace. He was taught the language of the Chaldeans and trained in many of the sciences of the Babylonian empire. He was to be groomed for training in government and would sit to eat at the "king's table"—to eat as did royalty, eating things abhorrent to the Jewish dietary law.

*Explain how this lesson shows that God has a desire for his children to remain true to His commandments and faithful to their convictions—regardless of surroundings, culture, or the actions of others. Daniel was able to stand because he settled the question of principles long before he was taken captive. Once we determine to live our lives by principles, we can let our principles navigate our lives. Choices and decisions become fewer and easier.*

**Questions to ask your class:**
1) **Why was it important to Daniel that he not "eat the king's meat?" Do you think it was important to God that Daniel not do so?**

2) Did Daniel's captivity make his character or reveal it? Why?
3) How did Daniel approach those in authority above him with his problem? What can we learn from him in dealing with similar situations in our own lives?

## Main Points
- The depth of our commitment is revealed by what it takes to stop us.
- Having the courage of our commitments comes by mental assent--purposing.

The depth of our commitment is
revealed by what it takes to STOP us.

# LESSON 22

## Great Characters of The Bible

*Introduction: This lesson is about three young men whose faith allowed them to stand together while standing apart. They are better known to us as the three Hebrew children—Shadrach, Meshach, and Abednego. We are often called to be different when the world is pressing us to conform, but Hananiah, Mishael, and Azariah learned that sometimes God allows us to go through "the fire" while standing for what is right. Sometimes God wants us to go through trial, for the lesson we learn "in the fire" is far greater than the lesson learned by avoiding it.*

### Hananiah, Mishael, Azariah

**Background Reading: Daniel 3:1-30
Text: Daniel 3: 1-30; Key Verses: Daniel 3:16-18; 3: 23-25; 3: 28-30**

Main Emphasis—Learning how to "go through the fire" for right's sake

History—Hananiah, Mishael, and Azariah were companions of Daniel. They, like he, were sons of royalty in Jerusalem that had been brought captive to Babylon to learn the ways of their captors in order to serve them. They, along with Daniel, had refused to eat the king's meat and thus kept themselves pure upon their arrival. Now, Nebuchadnezzar had built an idol of gold—a huge totem pole, if you will. At the sound of the orchestra, all were to fall down and worship it. Those who would refuse would be burned. When all fell in obeisance to the idol, Hananiah, Mishael, and Azariah refused.

*Explain how this lesson shows that standing for God and right does not always mean that deliverance from all hardship is guaranteed for the Christian. In fact, Paul (writing to Timothy) says "Yea, and all that will live godly in Christ Jesus shall suffer persecution." 2 Tim. 3:12. The lessons that can be learned going "through the fire" are important ones. How else could their faith have been tested? Christianity is more than a parachute or an escape clause in a contract. It is a relationship of trust between a believer and the Saviour.*

**Questions to ask your class:**
1) **Did these young men not have a right to defend themselves? Why didn't they?**
2) **What is the most important lesson learned from this story? Explain why.**

## Main Points
- **While "fires" are not from God, the lessons to be learned from them are.**
- **Having faith even when it seems our faith may have failed.**

# LESSON 23

## Great Characters of The Bible

*Introduction: This lesson is about a man of God who was asked to sacrifice his reputation so that God could teach the people of Israel a truth that they needed to learn. So often we would do the will of God, as long as it is convenient. Hosea was a "minor" prophet—only in that his writings were of a short nature. His mission was "major"—to show the people of Israel the awfulness of their sin and its effect in a vivid way.*

### Hosea

**Background Reading: Hosea 1-3**
**Text:  Hosea 1: 1-9; 3: 1-5; Key Verses: Hosea 3:1-5**

Main Emphasis—Losing ourselves in the cause of Christ, and losing our sin as well

History—Hosea was one of the longest serving prophets (through the reigns of Uzziah, Jotham, Ahaz, Hezekiah, and

Joash.) The main thrust of the book is God's command to Hosea to take a wife of "whoredoms." This was done to be used as an object lesson to show the people their sin against God as a parallel to the marriage of a Godly prophet with a harlot. The names of the children are important. Jezreel means "God sows"—referring to judgment; Loruhamah means "no mercy"; Loammi means "not my people."

*Explain how this lesson depicts in such graphic detail the effects of sin on our relationship with God. We, as God's people, are set apart. James 4:4 says, "Ye adulterers and adulteresses, know ye not that the friendship of the world is enmity with God? whosoever therefore will be a friend of the world is the enemy of God." The strength of this statement testifies of the importance of holiness before God. God will not forever "wink" at sin. Sin in our lives brings separation—from God! (See Isaiah 59:2.) As the most definitive definition of Hell is "eternal separation from God", sin in our lives brings Hell to us, as Christians (who hold on to our sins.)*

**Questions to ask your class:**

1) What aspect of Hosea's life did God ask him to sacrifice? How can we apply this today?
2) How can Christians experience Hell on earth? How can we avoid it?

## Main Points
- **Sacrifice is not measured by what we have left, but by our willingness to obey.**
- **Sin separates from God—now for the Christian; through eternity for the lost.**

# THE CAUSE IS JUST

# LESSON 24

## Great Characters of The Bible

*Introduction: This lesson is about a man of God who decided he no longer wanted to do the will of God. It might be asked how a man who "ran from God" could have any character traits worth studying, but God saw fit to give him a second chance...and he took it. Many times we look at disobedience before obedience and see only the disobedience. This lesson should be an inspiration for those who think that perhaps God has passed them by.*

### Jonah

**Background Reading: Jonah 1-4**
**Text: Jonah 3:1-10; Key Verses: Jonah 3:1-3**

Main Emphasis—Disobedience followed by repentance and obedience is still obedience.

History—Jonah's story is well known. The

great fish that God prepared to swallow Jonah after Jonah's flight from God's will was real. The story is not a parable. Having sought to "flee from the presence of God", Jonah set sail on a passenger ship and through a great storm he was thrown overboard and swallowed by a great fish. He was there for three days and three nights, eventually praying and giving God the praise for all that was happening. The great fish spat Jonah up on dry ground and he went preaching unto Nineveh. A great revival ensued and God spared the city.

*Explain how this lesson shows that 1) we cannot run from God 2) God disciplines His children 3) the proper response to chastisement is praise 4) God is the God of a second chance and 5) doing God's will eventually is better than not doing God's will at all. Jonah's strength came in the fact that (even with an improper attitude at times) he recognized the influence of God in his life, and chose rather to obey Him when again given the chance.*

**Questions to ask your class:**
1) **Why did Jonah think he could run from the presence of God? Could he?**

2) Chapter 2 deals with Jonah's prayer in the fish's belly. What did he learn there?

## Main Points
- It is better to disobey, repent, and obey than to give lip service alone to obedience.
- If God could not use sinners, He could use no one.

Running from God is poor exercise for the weak Christian.

# LESSON 25

# Great Characters of The Bible

*Introduction: This lesson involves the man whose name is synonymous with patience. The Book of Job is considered to be oldest writing in Scripture. Job, the man, lived sometime around the time of Abraham. He was considered to be the wealthiest man of his time, as well as the most Godly. In James 5:11 we find the following words: "Behold, we count them happy which endure. Ye have heard of the patience of Job, and have seen the end of the Lord; that the Lord is very pitiful, and of tender mercy." He was a real man who faced real problems in as recorded on The Book of Job.*

## Job

**Background Reading: Job 1:1-22
Text: Job 1:1-22; Key Verses: Job 1:1; Job 1:22**

Main Emphasis—Remaining faithful

through testing

History—While Job is regarded to the wealthiest man of his time, God considered him a spiritual success. God presented Satan with him as a choice candidate for faithfulness to God. Satan accused God of protecting Job by building a hedge around him (which was true) and that by removing it, Job would curse God (which was not true.) Thus began the trials and testings of Job. He lost family, health and wealth. How he reacted is a testimony to his faithfulness to God and to his character.

*Explain how this lesson deals with several important areas that have an impact on our lives today: 1) that it is God who protects the Christian from Satan's destruction, 2) that Satan must receive the permission of God before he can ever put a Christian through the fires of testing, and 3) that God only allows testing in the lives of His children whom He explicitly trusts. James 1:13 states "Let no man say when he is tempted, I am tempted of God: for God cannot be tempted with evil, neither tempteth he any man." We know that testing never comes from God, but rather that He allows Satan to perform it at His (God's) discretion.*

**Questions to ask your class:**
1) What did Job lose? Job 42:10-15 records the final chapter. What did he regain?
2) Look up Romans 5:3. What does this verse teach and how does it relate to Job'

## Main Points
- Trials and tribulations serve only to make us better or prepare us to help others.
- Faithfulness through trials yields God's blessings.

*The winds of adversity do not build character—they simply reveal it.*

# LESSON 26

## Great Characters of The Bible

*Introduction: This lesson involves a young lady whose virtue is unquestioned, an uncle whose encouragement is unwavering, and an enemy whose villainy is unending...until God Himself through a miraculous series of events put an end to this amazing drama. Though the name of God is nowhere to be found in the entire book of Esther, His Hand of Providence is found everywhere. It is a story of heroism, courage, faith, and trust in God to take care of us as we move through the circumstances of life. It is a Biblical Cinderella-like story.*

### Esther

**Background Reading: Esther 1-4, preferably the entire book**
**Text: Esther 1:7-2:10; Key Verses: Esther 2:9-10; Esther 4:14**

Main Emphasis—Standing for right when called upon to do so

History—King Ahasuerus was the wicked king of the Media-Persian Empire at this time of Jewish captivity. He, in one of his drunken feasts, commanded Queen Vashti to appear before his guests to reveal her beauty to them. Upon her refusal, King Ahasuerus dethroned her and started a search for a new queen. Every fair young maiden was paraded before him, and he chose Esther. Upon her choice, Mordecai, her uncle, counseled her not to reveal her Jewish heritage. It proved a wise decision for later she was called upon to deliver her people from a wickedly devised death sentence by Haaman, Mordecai's arch enemy.

*Explain how this lesson shows that each of us has a place in the economy of God and that none of us are here by chance or mistake. So many times we feel that we cannot make a difference in this life, yet God has a place and a plan for us in that place. Each of us will face at some point in our lives "such a time as this", where what we say, think, or care about will make a difference if only we act upon the courage of our convictions. Character is revealed not in what we can accomplish many times, but in what we allow God to accomplish through us.*

**Questions to ask your class:**
1) Was Mordecai's counsel to not reveal herself as a Jew cowardice? Why or why not?
2) What are some ways we can apply this lesson to our lives today? What is our "such a time?"

## Main Points
- Each of us has a purpose in God's plan—we need to seek to fulfill that purpose.
- Standing for right when it counts must become second-nature to us.

# LESSON 27

## Great Characters of The Bible

*Introduction: This lesson involves the first in a study of the Apostles. While Matthew was not the first chosen, and little is said about him, the Lord chose him to be the human instrument responsible for the penning of the first book of the New Testament. While the book of Matthew deals with the Saviour as King, it could be thought quite unusual that this former tax collector should be given the honor of such writing. If man were the author the Scriptures, he probably would have had a Jewish scholar as the writer of the first book of the New Testament.*

## Matthew

**Background Reading: Luke 5:27-29, Acts 1:13**
**Text: Luke 5:27-29, Acts 1:13; Key Verses: Luke 5:28-29, Acts 1:13**

Main Emphasis—Leaving it all for Jesus

and staying away from it 'all'

History—Matthew, who was also known as Levi, was a publican...a tax collector. These men were the tools of Rome that Rome used to excise taxes from the Jewish citizenry. They were commonly known as being dishonest, ruthless, thieves, and generally despised. When Jesus came to Matthew's place of work, He was criticized. He had just finished healing the palsied man, and the Pharisees were watching Him. When Matthew left all and followed Jesus, he made a feast for Jesus—with many publicans in attendance. Matthew reached those whom he knew best...his worldly friends.

*Explain how this lesson shows that commitment to Christ is just that... commitment. In this time of such weak commitment to the cause of Christ—lack of love for the house of God, the desire to remain in sin while called upon to be holy, the mixture of the world's tastes into the church, the lack of Biblical standards among even Christian leadership, etc., it is refreshing to see a man who left all and never went back to it. What Christianity is lacking today is the person who sees commitment as real—something for which to stand.*

**Questions to ask your class:**
1) **Why do we today regard commitment so lightly? Does our environment dictate our obedience?**
2) **Why has the church of today lost its holiness? How can we live separated lives?**

## Main Points
- **God is seeking for those whose commitment is not determined by environment.**
- **The seriousness of our commitment is revealed by what it takes to derail us.**

# LESSON 28

## Great Characters of The Bible

*Introduction: This lesson involves the most well-known of all the Apostles—the Apostle Peter. He is known for his zealous attitude and his sometimes hasty words. No doubt he was a passionate man who sometimes spoke before he thought, but he was one with whom you knew where you stood. We could look at his zeal and certainly emulate that, but in this lesson we will be observing that which makes Peter tick—his boldness.*

## Peter

**Background Reading: Matthew 4:18-20, Matthew 16:13-18, Acts 4:8-13**
**Text: Acts 4:8-13; Key Verses: Acts 4:8, 13**

Main Emphasis—Learning the lesson of boldness in our witnessing

History—Simon Peter was the most colorful of all Christ's disciples. He was zealous, bold, hasty, and quite a talker. Simon Peter is rebuked more than any other of the Apostles for his words. He seemed to always be saying something to get himself in trouble. He was impulsive, for it was he who cut off the high priest's servant's ear in the Garden. It was he who walked on water, then needed to be rescued. It was he who denied Jesus three times, but it was also he who wept bitterly because of it and repented. It was he who was used to deliver the Pentecostal sermon. According to tradition, Peter was later crucified upside down (not counting himself worthy to be crucified as Jesus was.)

*Explain how this lesson shows that boldness is an element of our witnessing that is accomplished by the power of the Holy Spirit. It is the Holy Spirit that grants such boldness. If we use the excuse that we have no boldness in witnessing, we are simply admitting that we have no Holy Spirit power on our ministry. As it is the ministry of every Christian to tell others of Jesus' love, let us seek the Holy Spirit's power so that we may proceed with boldness. Peter exemplified this (not because of his personality) because he was surrendered to the Holy Spirit's leading.*

Questions to ask your class:
1) What aspects of Peter's life are worth modeling ourselves after? How can we be bold as Peter was bold?
2) Who is the Giver of boldness? Can we witness effectively without His power?

## Main Points
- Holy Spirit boldness is necessary for fruitful witnessing.
- Boldness is not based on our personality, but rather upon our relationship—with God.

# LESSON 29

## Great Characters of The Bible

*Introduction: This lesson is intended to show the importance of diligence in the service of God, both prior to one's call and the need for it afterwards. God has always used busy people (Elisha, plowing the field; David, tending sheep; Moses, herding his father-in-law's herds; Gideon, threshing wheat; Peter, fishing, etc., etc.) Though we often wish to be used of God without the accompanying sacrifice of work, there is nothing that has ever been or ever will be accomplished in God's will without the willingness to work.*

### James

**Background Reading: Matt. 4:21-22, Mark 1:19-20, Luke 9:51-56, Acts 12:1-3 Text: Mark 1:19-20; Key Verse: Mark 1:20**

Main Emphasis—Diligence... a prerequisite to being used of God

History—James was a fisherman by trade.

He and his brother John were called the "Sons of Thunder" by Jesus. Luke 9: 51-56 gives an occasion of one of the instances where they earned this title. James was more than just a man with an explosive personality, he was a staunch supporter of Jesus Christ. He was part of the 'inner circle' (Peter, James, and John) and could be found in the most crucial and intimate settings. In our selection of Scripture, he was found doing the menial, yet important task of mending the nets. From before the time of his call, James was diligent.

*Explain how this lesson shows that diligence is a virtue that is almost lost in this "me-first", "instant" society in which we live. We have all but lost the ability to do the tedious and the necessary. So many people go through life today expecting things to be 'fun.' So quickly are they disappointed when they discover that no one has promised them that. We see this loss of diligence and ingenuity in our lack of Bible study (it's not fun enough!) We see it in our unwillingness to pray (that takes too much diligence!) Let us learn from James to incorporate diligence into our lives.*

**Questions to ask your class:**
1) Who could have been mending the nets? What does this reveal about James?
2) What are some 'tedious' spiritual things? Are they important to God? To us?

## Main Points
- **Diligence is a requirement in service for God.**
- **You can be diligent without being faithful, but you cannot be faithful without being diligent. Remember the difference and remember the danger!**

# LESSON 30

## Great Characters of The Bible

*Introduction: This lesson is intended to show the need of believing. Though John was an apostle of whom it was said that Jesus loved, it was not until the selected passage that he confirmed his own belief in Jesus' finished work as Messiah. In our background readings we find John at the trial of Jesus, at His Crucifixion, and afterward. The text gives us his conversion. When he saw that Jesus was raised from the dead, he believed. He would later, under the direction of the Holy Spirit, pen I John 5:13—without a doubt, the consummate verse on assurance.*

## John

**Background Reading: John 19:26-27, John 20:1-8, John 21:20-23**
**Text: John 20:1-8; Key Verse John 20:8**

Main Emphasis—The proof of belief is assurance.

History—John, the brother of James, was a fisherman by trade. He left all and followed Jesus, quickly developing a special relationship with the Saviour. He was part of the inner circle, the Apostle to live the longest—being exiled on the Isle of Patmos, after a burning in a caldron of boiling oil failed. He was called 'the disciple whom Jesus loved' and the "one who leaned on Jesus' breast." Both were affectionate names given to show Jesus' special love for him. He wrote (by the Holy Spirit's direction) The Gospel of John and the First, Second, and Third Epistles of John. He emphasized love and assurance in his writings.

*Explain how this lesson shows that assurance is not an elusive hope, but a verifiable doctrine. Salvation is God's plan of redemption for man back to God. Only He could accomplish it and only He can secure it. He leaves it up to us only to accept the grace which He freely gives to us through the sacrifice of His Own Dear Son. John saw this sacrifice first-hand and spent the rest of his natural life proclaiming the goodness and love of God that grants to us the complete assurance of our salvation.*

**Questions to ask your class:**
1) How do you think John's special relationship to Jesus may have affected his writings?
2) Why do you suppose John saved his salvation statement for this time?

## Main Points

- **Assurance is a fact that we can comprehend.**
- **The love of God will lead us to the acceptance of His plan of salvation—the faithfulness of God will keep us in that salvation, for eternity!**

# LESSON 31

# Great Characters of The Bible

*Introduction: This lesson is about one of the greatest men in the Bible. Even Jesus, in Matthew 11:11 and Luke 7:28, called John the Baptist the greatest man that ever lived. The focus of this lesson will not be on his 'greatness' of personality, but rather on his 'greatness' of character. Though we could focus on his boldness, his greatness in witnessing, and his dynamic personality and inspiring messages, there is one characteristic that the Saviour points to in this man's life that is worth remembering—humility.*

## John the Baptist

**Background Reading: Matthew 3:1-17 Text: John 3:22-32; Key Verse: John 3:30**

Main Emphasis—The most powerful ability is humility.

History—John the Baptizer, or John the Baptist as we know him best, was Jesus' second cousin. (Mary and John's mother, Elisabeth, were cousins.) His ministry was prophesied in the book of Malachi (Malachi 4:5-6). He was a bold proclaimer of the truth, baptized Jesus, preached against moral evil in government, was imprisoned for his preaching, and was beheaded as a reward for the dancing of Salome before King Herod. His practice of baptizing converts was how he got his surname, and it was adopted as the proper way to identify with this new religion of Christianity. His clothing and methodology were unusual (camel's hair, eating locusts and wild honey), but his message was plain, "Prepare ye the way of the Lord."

*Explain how this lesson shows that greatness is not always measured in accomplishments, but is also measured in attitude as well. Let us not miss out on the teaching that the greatest thing to be learned from his life was that he was a humble man. No one can see Christ clearly if he is full of himself, for self blocks and dims the purest view of the Saviour.*

Questions to ask your class:
1) Do you think being different is necessary for being right? Is it wrong to be different?
2) Why is it important to be humble? What is the opposite of humility?

## Main Points
- We cannot get a clear picture of God if we keep our eyes on ourselves.
- Humility is a virtue reserved for those who have seen themselves in the light of the Saviour, and acknowledge their standing without Him.

We cannot get a clear picture of God if we keep our eyes on ourselves.

# LESSON 32

## Great Characters of The Bible

*Introduction: This lesson is intended to show that God can still use those who have "blown it." How many Christians go through this life defeated because of something in their past? While it is true that God wants our first and our best, "He remembereth that we are dust." As with Jonah, Moses, Peter, and Jacob (to name but a few,) God can still use us even after we fail. While this lesson is not intended to endorse failure, it is intended to pick up after the failure and help the student (and teacher) realize that God still loves us when we fail and fall, and He still has a plan for our lives.*

### John Mark

**Background Reading: Acts 12:1-25; Acts 15:36-41; II Timothy 4:11**
**Text: Acts 15:36-41   Key Verse:  II Timothy 4:11**

Main Emphasis—Service beyond failure

History—John Mark was introduced to us in the famous episode of Peter's release from prison by the angel. The church was praying at Mary's house for Peter's release. This Mary was John Mark's mother, the sister of Barnabas. He went with Barnabas and Paul on their first mission tour, but left and went home (see Acts 15:38). When Barnabas wanted to take John Mark along the second time, Paul disagreed strongly and Barnabas wound up taking John Mark and Paul took Silas. Later, however, in a letter to Timothy, he asked that John Mark now be sent unto him—for he was profitable to Paul. John Mark, a convert of Peter's (see I Peter 5:13—refers to him as Marcus) recorded the Gospel of Mark.

*Explain how this lesson shows that failure, while devastating, is not necessarily the end. It is true that some things can never be the same. (Example: A pastor who divorces or commits adultery can never, Biblically, be a pastor again. He can, however, be a faithful member of a church.) Stress that personal holiness and doing right are always the best alternatives, but show that God is a God of mercy.*

Questions to ask your class:
1) Was John Mark a quitter? Have you ever quit on a commitment to God?
2) Why do you suppose John was profitable to Paul later on? Who changed?

## Main Points
- **Failure is a temporary setback, not a permanent surrender.**
- **The mercy of God is revealed in His willingness to forgive us when we sin and to restore to fellowship again with Him when we confess that sin (I John 1:9.)**

# LESSON 33

## Great Characters of The Bible

*Introduction: This lesson is intended to show that there is a place of service that sometimes is given to the Christian for which little notice is paid. We often remember with great admiration the great deeds of the 'great' Apostles, while overlooking the deeds of those who (though not greatly recognized for their efforts) were none-the-less still faithful. Such is the case with this man, Luke. In society, he was probably better recognized for his work as a physician of men's bodies, but his new love was the healing of men's souls.*

### Luke

**Background Reading: II Corinthians 13:14; Colossians 4:14**
**Text: II Timothy 4:11; Key Verse: Philemon 1:24**

Main Emphasis—Remaining faithful while working without recognition

History—It is commonly held that Luke was a convert of the Apostle Paul's, Paul having won him to the Lord in Antioch. Though Scripture is not clear on this, it is a plausible theory as Luke joined Paul again and again on his mission journeys as described in the book of Acts. (The Holy Spirit allowed Luke to write both the Gospel According to Luke, and The Acts of the Apostles.) Whether a convert of Paul, or a member of the first seventy disciples (as some propose,) he was definitely a faithful worker for the Gospel's sake, garnering little recognition along the way.

*Explain how this lesson shows that service does not have to 'appear' great in the eyes of men to be great. If recognition here were the reward for service to God, then God would recognize all here. To the laborer who remains faithful, God has promised reward. The most important attribute for the steward (the one who is entrusted with the Father's work) is "to be found faithful." Let us never look to circumstances to judge our work's worth to the Master; let us rather be faithful above the circumstances and, in turn, we shall be faithful to the One Who has called us to the work.*

Questions to ask your class:
1) Do you suppose it was difficult for a man of skill to get such little recognition?
2) What do you suppose Luke did to handle such a situation? How can we do the same?

## Main Points
- Service garners God's notice, not necessarily man's recognition.
- Do not judge the place your asked to labor by the attention you will receive, but rather by the task that needs your attention.

*Man's Recognition*

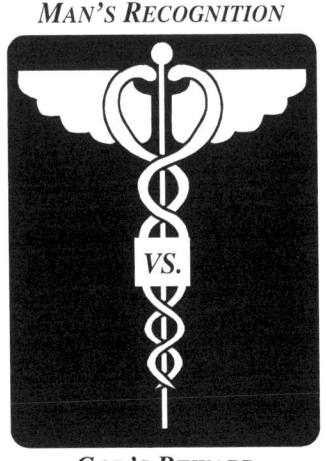

*God's Reward*

# LESSON 34

## Great Characters of The Bible

*Introduction: This lesson is for the "church kid." So often, in our attempts to find the best in the vessels of God's choosing, we neglect the most obvious source—the Christian home. We are falsely led to believe that God only uses those from tainted pasts in His work. The truth is that He would just as soon use the person who has grown up in Christianity, but too many have grown tired in their Christianity rather than having grown up in it. Timothy was a third generation Christian who successfully sought and found God's will for his life.*

## Timothy

**Background Reading: II Timothy 1:1-14 Text: II Timothy 1:1-6; Key Verse: II Timothy 1:5**

**Main Emphasis—Growing up in the faith—not growing out of it**

History—Timothy was the son of a converted Jewess named Eunice and an unnamed and probably lost Greek father. His grandmother, Lois, was also a Christian. Paul refers to him constantly as his "son in the faith." This was not because he led him to the Lord (Timothy was already a believer when Paul returned to Lystra,) but rather because Paul took Timothy and trained him in evangelism. Later Timothy would become the first bishop (or pastor) of the church at Ephesus (II Timothy 4:22.) His training as a pastor and encouragement from his mentor, Paul, are seen in the Epistles of I Timothy and II Timothy.

*Explain how this lesson shows that growing up in church, around the things of God does not necessarily mean that we have to grow cold because of our familiarity. It is not God's will that spiritual training be wasted because of "inside" information. Let us seek to portray the dynamic life as one that involves and thrives upon the teachings and lessons learned from close encounters with our Christian heritage. It is special to be used—it* **should** *be more* *common among those who are the most familiar with God's house.*

**Questions to ask your class:**
1) How can you relate to the "church-going" Timothy? Why do you think so many Christians grow "tired of" their faith instead of growing "up in" it?
2) How can we maintain our excitement about the things of God?

## Main Points
- **Familiarity should not breed contempt, but rather respect.**
- **Learn to grow up in your faith—not out of it!**

# LESSON 35

## Great Characters of The Bible

*Introduction: This lesson is intended for those who are sometimes left out in Sunday School lesson series—the married couple, seeking to do God's will. So often, we limit our stress of important training lessons to just the younger children or to the teenage audience. One of the key foundational building blocks of the successful local church is its ministry to and for married couples. We can learn a great deal about the maturity, zeal for learning, and desire to communicate their faith from this important couple. Paul, the Apostle, refers to them on several occasions—always commending their faith and example.*

### Aquila and Priscilla

**Background Reading: Acts 18:1-28; Romans 16:3; I Corinthians 16:19**
**Text: Acts 18:24-28; Key Verse: Acts 18:26**

Main Emphasis—Passing on sound doctrine

History—Aquila and Priscilla were tentmakers by occupation, residing in Corinth. They had been forced to leave their adopted Rome (Aquila was originally from Pontus, Galatia) because of the decree of Claudius Caesar, which had forced all Jews to leave the capital city. They had migrated to Corinth, a rich port city of Greece across the Ionian Sea. There they tended to their trade and attended the local Jewish synagogue. Aquila and Priscilla were saved when Paul came through Corinth and preaching Jesus as Messiah, and later had a church in their own home.

*Explain how this lesson shows that there is definitely a ministry in the church for those who seize the opportunities to disciple new believers. When this new convert to Christianity, Apollos, came to faith in Christ, it was through the teaching ministry of Aquila and Priscilla that he came to a more excellent knowledge of the Scriptures. They sought not to oppose him for his lack of knowledge, but rather they took Apollos "under their wing" so that he might learn. This is a necessary part of the church. We may win all the lost we possibly can, but if we fail to disciple those new converts, we have failed them.*

**Questions to ask your class:**
1) How can we seek to be like Aquila and Priscilla? Why does Scripture record this?
2) Name some ways that you could possibly be a "discipler."

## Main Points
- **Faith is essential for salvation; passing that faith on is essential for survival.**
- **Maturing in the Word brings the need for discipling others in the Word.**

*Salvation, Separation, Soul-winning*

# LESSON 36

## Great Characters of The Bible

*Introduction: This lesson is given to show us the importance of always having a teachable spirit. Apollos was a gifted man who could have looked at his gifts and thought that he had 'arrived' spiritually. He possessed a character trait that each of us should strive to maintain in our own lives. We need to be teachable. It has often been said that since all men know something that we do not, that all men are our teachers. Apollos was a good example of this character quality. We should never get to the point in our Christian walk where we think that we know too much to learn.*

### Apollos

**Background Reading: Acts 18: 24-19:1; I Corinthians 3: 1-7**
**Text: Acts 18: 24-28; Key Verses: Acts 18: 27-28**

Main Emphasis—Learning in our maturity

History—Apollos was a Jew who was born in Alexandria, Egypt. He was converted to Christianity as a disciple of John the Baptist. Having read and studied the Scriptures, he sought out to preach and teach the message of the Messiah to his fellow Jews. Upon coming to Corinth, he met Aquila and Priscilla. They brought him aside and expounded unto him the full revelation of the Gospel as Paul had taught them. Apollos, upon hearing of this doctrine, responded properly and sought to learn as much as Aquila and Priscilla could teach him. He continued in Bible studies with them until leaving Corinth, better prepared to teach others.

*Explain how this lesson shows that no matter how long we have been a Christian or how many church services and Sunday School classes we have attended, we still never have the right to think that we have arrived spiritually. Much like the sponge that has been soaked in water and set off to the side, eventually drying up, so is the Christian who thinks he or she has no more need of teaching. The sponge will dry up and so will we. We would never think of eating until we were full and never eating again. We need to be willing to be constantly teachable.*

**Questions to ask your class:**
1) How can we be teachable today? What do we mean by being teachable?
2) Are there limits to 'new' knowledge? If so, what should be the standard of those limits?

## Main Points
- **Teachability is more important than teaching ability.**
- **Maturing spiritually is never to be confused with dying spiritually.**

Teachability is more important than teaching ability.

# LESSON 37

## Great Characters of The Bible

*Introduction: This lesson is given to those of us, who at times, think that we have 'blown it.' This is not about those times we just made an error in judgment, but when we really made a mistake that we thought could not be corrected. So often we find ourselves wrapping up and hiding in the problem itself that we see no chance for a solution at all. This can be seen in the child who eats the chocolate cookie and lies with crumbs all over his face to his mother, hiding the remainder safely behind his back. This lesson will show us what to do when we have done wrong.*

### Onesimus

**Background Reading: Philemon; Colossians 4:9**
**Text: Philemon; Key Verses: Philemon 1:11; Colossians 4:9**

Main Emphasis—Recovering from wrong

doing

History—Onesimus was a slave and a slave under Roman law had little to no rights, so when he made the mistake of stealing from his master and then compounding it by running away, he thought he was to be a fugitive for the rest of his life. He then met Paul who introduced him to Jesus, and his life was turned around. The reality of a genuine conversion to Jesus Christ is that it does not take away the consequences of our past actions—Jesus forgives us while people may not. Onesimus was in such a situation. He now was a believer (as was his master) and he went back to settle the score.

*Explain how this lesson shows that we must have the courage to face the consequences of our own actions. We must take responsibility and then seek to make the wrong right. Onesimus could have kept running, but his problems would not have gone away. Until we turn and learn to face problems head on, we will be forced to live with the guilt and confusion that comes from avoidance. Onesimus knew that it would not be easy, but then, whoever came up with the notion that things must be easy in life was mistaken. True joy comes from complete obedience.*

**Questions to ask your class:**
1) **In what ways can we be responsible for our actions today? Why is it important to be so?**
2) **How does taking responsibility remove guilt?**

## Main Points
- **Responsibility is taking control of our lives by facing our problems.**
- **True joy comes from complete obedience.**

---

The measure of a man's compassion
is his ability to forgive, but the measure
of his maturity is his ability to forgive himself.

# LESSON 38

## Great Characters of The Bible

*Introduction: This lesson is given to help those of us who, at times, have battled with the problem of doubt—which means that this is a lesson for all of us. While we remember the Apostle Peter for his rash and impetuous statements, he had a companion who almost equaled him—Thomas. Known and labeled for his doubting statements, it was also this same Thomas who asked important questions that some may have feared to ask of the Saviour and it was he who uttered the famous confession of "My Lord and My God!"*

## Thomas

**Background Reading: John 20:24-31; John 21:2; Acts 1:13**
**Text: John 20:24-31; Key Verses: John 20:28; Acts 1:13**

Main Emphasis—Recovering from doubt

History—Thomas, who was called

Didymus, was so called because his name means twin. Many have mistakenly thought that Didymus must surely mean "doubter," but it does not. Thomas was a disciple of Jesus. We first meet him when Jesus tells His disciples that He must return to Bethany (upon hearing of Lazarus' sickness and eventual death.) Bethany meant danger to Jesus and Thomas' attitude was, "We might as well die with Him…"— not exactly the most optimistic of the disciples. He would later see Jesus face to face after the Resurrection and that encounter would have a lasting effect on any doubts he may have ever had.

*Explain how this lesson shows that there are both hope and cure for the doubts we sometimes will face. When Thomas declared that he would not believe until he had seen the risen Lord and touched the wounds for himself, he was simply revealing that side of his faith from which all of us suffer—unbelief. Unbelief is a part of our faith because we are human. So often we forget that and fail to forgive ourselves for only being natural. While Jesus encouraged Thomas to believe without seeing, He still recognized the fact* *that Thomas **was** believing. The most important lesson to learn was that Thomas continued in the faith, after recovering from his doubt.*

**Questions to ask your class:**
1) **If whatever is not of faith is sin, how can we deal with doubt? Is perfect faith required?**
2) **How do we know that Thomas recovered from his doubts? What lesson can we learn?**

## Main Points
- **Recovering from doubt teaches more lessons than doubtless faith.**
- **Learning from your mistake is more important to God than the mistake itself.**

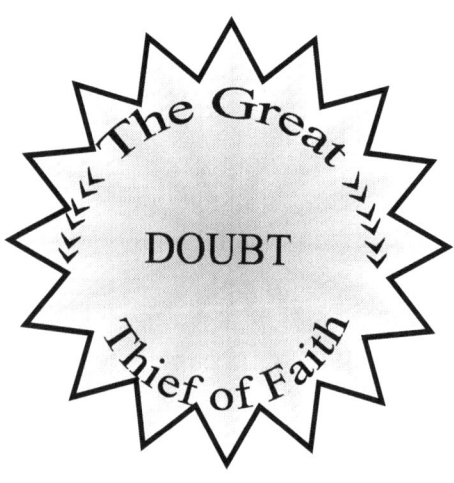

# LESSON 39

## Great Characters of The Bible

*Introduction: One of the most interesting true stories in the New Testament surely has to be the one of Philip and the Ethiopian eunuch. It has all the ingredients of drama—despair, hope, mystery, and resolution. We often focus on the recipient of grace in this story, and rightfully so—there is no greater story than grace in action. We sometimes neglect the messenger of that grace. Philip the Evangelist was such an instrument and we can learn some valuable lessons regarding evangelism and personal witnessing from this surrendered servant.*

### Philip, the Evangelist

**Background Reading: Acts 6:5; Acts 8:5-40**
**Text: Acts 8:5-30; Key Verses: Acts 8:29-30**

Main Emphasis—Learning the lessons of

evangelism

History—There are three Philips mentioned in the Bible. The first is the Apostle Philip; the second is Philip the Tetrarch, brother to Herod (whom Herod had taken Philip's wife in adultery and was opposed by John the Baptist—for which he later lost his head); the third is Philip the Deacon/Evangelist. The third Philip is the one we will be studying. He, along with Stephen and five others, were chosen to be the first deacons in Scripture. His zeal for evangelism was seen later in Acts by holding great evangelistic meetings and in his personal encounter with the Ethiopian eunuch. He would later settle in Caesarea and raise a family, continuing to be faithful to the end.

*Explain how this lesson reveals how to be an effective witness for Christ. We find Philip first being engaged in being found faithful. God then calls him to the office of a deacon and then to evangelism. He was obedient to the direct leading of the Holy Spirit, going when told to go and having the answers for the questioning Ethiopian.*

*He used wisdom in his approach and was courteous in his dealings. These are valuable lessons for anyone who wishes to be used of God in this area of public evangelism as well as personal soul-winning.*

**Questions to ask your class:**
1) What lessons can we learn in being a soul-winner from Phillip?
2) Do you believe that personal soul-winning is a calling or a responsibility? Or both?

## Main Points
- To be used, we first must be faithful.
- We cannot evaluate the assignments of God—they are all important to Him.

WHATEVER THE LANGUAGE

Ευαγγελλιον

TELL THE MESSAGE

# LESSON 40

## Great Characters of The Bible

*Introduction: This lesson is given as an example of choosing the "needful" things of God—worship. So often we choose to think that worship is not a necessary part of our Christian lives. We have feared it because of man-made notions of formality or unruliness. We look at those who call their festivities "worship" and are afraid to learn to worship God. Worship is not something reserved for children or just adults or for some Christians only—it is needful for all of us. From the nursery to the Senior Adults we need to worship God. Besides, God needs worship as much as we need to give it to Him.*

## Mary of Bethany

**Background Reading:** John 11:1-46; Luke 10:38-42
**Text:** Luke 10:38-42; **Key Verses:** Luke 10:38, 42

Main Emphasis—Learning the lesson of

worship

History—Lazarus, Mary, and Martha were some of Jesus' closet friends while He lived here among us. He would often stop in Bethany to visit and teach His friends there. There are four Marys in the Bible: Mary, the mother of Jesus; Mary Magdalene; Mary of Bethany (the one we are studying in this lesson); and Mary, greeted by Paul in the Epistle to the Romans. Mary's personality was one of quiet reflection and adoration for Jesus. It was she who took the precious ointment and anointed Jesus for his burial, wiping His feet with her hair. She was more concerned with Jesus than housework.

*Explain how this lesson teaches that there are times to come away from the normal activities of life and to simply sit at the feet of Jesus and take in His Word. While Mary of Bethany had the privilege of doing this in person while Jesus was upon the earth, she could only do it when He was with her physically. Today, we have a greater opportunity to worship at Jesus' feet. He can be with us at all times, and is. We simply need to get to the point in our lives where we acknowledge His presence and worship Him.*

**Questions to ask your class:**
1) How did Mary worship Jesus? Name at least three ways.
2) How can you and I worship Jesus today? Why is it better for us today than it was then?

## Main Points
- **Taking time apart with Jesus is better than having time take us apart.**
- **Worship is a not suggested practice for Christians—it is necessary.**

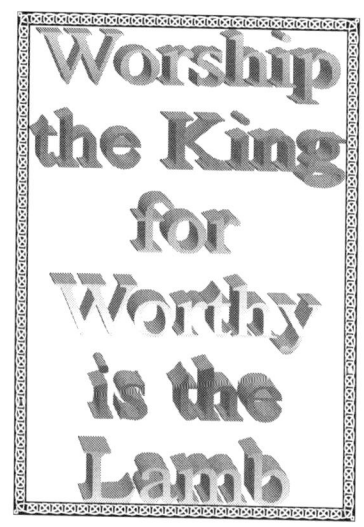

# LESSON 41

## Great Characters of The Bible

*Introduction: This lesson contains a very missing ingredient in our Christian community—service. Jesus once scolded Martha for worrying about temporal things when eternal things were more important, but He never rebuked her for possessing the characteristic of service. Because of a misunderstanding of that phrase we have often devalued the "menial" services that must be performed. Just because we do not see these services as important, does not mean that they are unimportant. The church today needs people who will just do "the work"—like Martha.*

## Martha

**Background Reading: John 11:1-57; Luke 10:38-42**
**Text: John 11:17-28; Key Verses: John 11:20, 28**

Main Emphasis—Learning the lessons of

service

History—Whenever Jesus would travel through Bethany, it was a known fact that He would be welcome in the home of Martha, Mary, and Lazarus. Whenever the Scripture records anything at all about Martha, it always records a record of her willingness to work. It was she who would be first to leave her chores for the Master, the first to express her feelings, the first to return to work, and the last to leave the job undone. Whatever else can be said about her record in Scripture, we are sure of this one thing—she had a servant's heart.

*Explain how this lesson shows that we, in order to "get the job done," must be willing to simply do the work. Sometimes we glamorize church and Christian service to the point where no one feels "called" or "qualified" without a mountain top experience. It is a shame that we do not emphasize the need for Christians who have a will to work. Nothing gets done without work—and that is true in the church as well as everyday life.*

*Ecclesiastes 9:10 says, "Whatsoever thy hand findeth to do, do it with thy might" and that is just what Martha was doing. Let us seek to do the job at hand with whatever God has given us, as a servant would.*

**Questions to ask your class:**
1) **How did Martha serve God and others? How can we serve God and others today?**
2) **What special calling did Martha need?**

## Main Points
- **Service is simply doing the job at hand, when the job needs done.**
- **God accepts volunteers as well as draftees.**

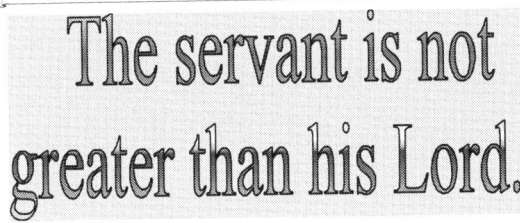

# LESSON 42

## Great Characters of The Bible

*Introduction: This lesson is about the need for faithful people. These are those who, for the most part, are unsung heroes and heroines of the faith. They sing in our choirs, teach our Sunday School classes, watch our children in the nurseries, fill the pews and are faithful to simply be there. This lesson is about more than simple duty. It is about the commitment to that duty—regardless of recognition or reward. The promise of the Saviour is that they shall someday be rewarded for their faithfulness.*

### Lydia

**Background Reading: Acts 16:11-40
Text: Acts 16:11-15; Key Verses: Acts 16:15, 40**

Main Emphasis—Bringing our faith to the workplace and the home

History—Lydia was a convert to

Christianity who just happened to be a business woman as well. This same chapter introduces us to a young Timothy, reveals Paul's Macedonian vision, records the salvation of the Philippian jailer, and tells of Paul's appeal to Caesar. Lydia's role could be lost in such important events, but this lady from Thyatira (one the seven cities mentioned in Revelation's seven churches) becomes important because of her example of faith in the workplace and in her home.

*Explain how this lesson shows that our faith is vital not only in a personal relationship, but in public activities as well. Whether it is the workplace or the schoolroom, faithfulness to God and to His work should not only be an intregal part of our lives—it should be the main focal point. Lydia was a stranger in a foreign city. Philippi was not her home, but she sought to be faithful there. Her workplace was a riverside and she sought to be faithful there. She desired to have Luke, Paul and Silas enter her home so that she could meet their needs at that time. She sought to be faithful there. After all, when she got saved, Scripture records that her household did as well.*

**Questions to ask your class:**
1) In what ways can we be faithful to our faith in the workplace or at school? Why is it important to be so?
2) How does maintaining the same level of public faithfulness as our private faithfulness increase our faith?

## Main Points
- Our faith cannot survive in a vacuum of self-indulgence—it must be shared publicly to thrive privately.
- Faith that is not a part of our everyday lives is a faith that will depart in our every day problems.

---

# *HOME, SCHOOL WORK, PLAY*

### *LIVE A LIFE OF FAITH DAY BY DAY*

# LESSON 43

# Great Characters of The Bible

*Introduction: This lesson is given to help remind us of the great characteristic of forgiveness that God displays toward us. Mary Magdalene was a woman who had been touched by the Saviour in a miraculous way. The character trait which she displays that is worth our notice is that she understood her forgiveness. It is one thing to be forgiven and quite another to understand that forgiveness. The key to that understanding was that she did not forget from whence she had come, Who had made the difference in her life, and that even death could not diminish the relationship sustained by her gratitude.*

## Mary Magdalene

**Background Reading: Luke 8:1-3; Mark 15:40-41, 16:9-11; John 20:11-18**
**Text: John 20:11-18; Key Verses: Luke 8:2-3; Mark 15:40; John 20:16-17**

Main Emphasis—Understanding forgiveness

History—Throughout history, Mary Magdalene has been known in Christian circles as a fallen woman. Nowhere in Scripture is this borne out to be factual. Magdala, the country from which she came, was quite renowned for the great number of prostitutes there. That fact does not necessarily mean that she was of that profession. Scripture only says that she had seven devils cast out of her. Whatever her former life was, it was very evident that meeting the Master changed her forever. From a forgiven sinner to a redeemed follower, Mary Magdalene was one of the most loyal persons in Jesus' ministry.

*Explain how this lesson shows the importance of appreciating our standing in Jesus Christ. Psalm 40:2 says "He brought me up also out of an horrible pit, out of the miry clay, and set my feet upon a rock, and established my goings." Too often, we tend to forget how much Jesus has done for us. We get so far from our past that we fail to thank the One Who made our future. Mary Magdalene knew she was a sinner, forgiven by the Saviour. She was faithful in His ministry, His Crucifixion, His death and eventual Resurrection.*

**Questions to ask your class:**
1) How did Mary Magdalene show her gratitude?  Why is it important to be grateful?
2) What are some ways we can remember our past?

## Main Points
- **Gratitude is more than thankfulness—it is an attitude of gratefulness.**
- **Remembering whence we came can keep us straight in the way we are going.**

# LESSON 44

# Great Characters of The Bible

*Introduction: This lesson is all about the responsibility that we as Christians today practice less and less. Andrew was a soul-winner, a leader of people to Christ. That is what soul-winning is all about—just bringing those you meet in everyday situations to meet the Master. There are no special traits that Andrew is said to possess. He simply saw those he met as in need—in need of the Saviour Whom he himself had met. Whether we are in the first grade, the last year of college, or settled in our professions, Andrew is the Scriptural example of the soul-winner who was soul-conscious.*

## Andrew

**Background Reading:** John 1:37-42; John 6:5-9; John 12:20-22
**Text:** John 1:37-42; **Key Verses:** John 1:41-42; John 12:22

Main Emphasis—Discipleship in action

History—Andrew, along with his more famous brother Peter, was a simple fisherman. Jesus met him on the seashore one day and showed Himself as the Messiah for whom Andrew had been waiting. He left his nets that day and fulfilled the promise that Jesus had made him—he would now be a fisher of men. His first convert was his brother, Simon. Where would the early church have been without that first convert? Who would have preached the great sermon at Pentecost if Andrew had not been soul-conscious?

*Explain how this lesson shows that we must take the command to witness seriously. In all of the Scriptures that were read, Andrew is found introducing someone to Jesus. First it was his brother Peter, then the boy with the loaves and fishes, and then the Greeks who sought to meet Jesus. Soul-winning is more than a command; it is a lifestyle of constant awareness and witnessing. Soul-winning needs to be done in school, at church, at home, in the work place—anywhere we meet people. It is simply introducing someone to Jesus—He does the rest!*

**Questions to ask your class:**
1) To whom does the command to witness apply? How can we fulfill that commandment?
2) Who do you know that has never met Jesus? What can you do about that?

## Main Points
- **Soul-winning is an awareness of others' destinies and sharing the Good News.**
- **True love for others does not wait for an opportunity—it creates one.**

# LESSON 45

# Great Characters of The Bible

*Introduction: This lesson is given to those of us, who at times, think that we have no place in the service of God after salvation. Too often, we seem to think that only preachers or evangelists or deacons have the ability to do God's will. While those offices do require special requirements as outlined in God's Word, there is something that all Christians can and should do—witness to the lost and dying world around us. No one could have come from a background of sin as easily as this woman whom we know only as "The Woman at the Well."*

## The Woman at the Well

**Background Reading: John 4:1-42**
**Text: John 4:1-30; Key Verses: John 4:28-29**

Main Emphasis—Sharing the good news with excitement

History—Jesus had separated Himself from His disciples as they had gone to buy food. He was leaving Judea and going to Galilee by means of Samaria. This was not a normal route for Jews, but Jesus "must needs go through Samaria." This was because He knew He would be meeting the woman at the well. She was a Samaritan, and had come daily to draw water from the well there. What she did not know was that this Man she would meet would change her life forever. Unmarried, living with a man who was not her husband, and having had five husbands before this time, she was "ripe unto harvest."

*Explain how this lesson shows that once we are saved there is a natural desire to share with others the "good news" of what Jesus has done in our lives. So it was with this woman. She immediately went into town to tell others of this Jesus who became her Saviour. Many were saved by her testimony and the Bible records this in a fashion to remind us of our need for zeal. She brought the message of salvation to others that needed it. When we think that we can do nothing for God, or God surely cannot use us because we have been so sinful, we need to remember the Samaritan woman at the well—she witnessed to others immediately.*

**Questions to ask your class:**
1) What does this lesson teach about God's ability to use us?
2) What is our responsibility in witnessing?

## Main Points
- No one has ever been saved by a silent witness.
- Some people have no witness because they have never experienced salvation.

WHEN THE HAND OF FORGIVENESS TOUCHES THE HAND OF NEED, HOPE IS STIRRED AND GRATITUDE IS BORN.

# Also Available from the Author

BUFFET of the MIND  ISBN: 1608131483
PublishAmerica                        2009

*Buffet of the Mind* is a collection of poetry styles on a variety of subjects. The reader will find forms such as haiku, senryu, sonnets, tankas, dodoitsu, and many more. It will allow the reader to be introduced to new and exciting forms while exploring classic favorites as well. *Buffet of the Mind* is written for the causal reader as well as the poetry buff. It covers themes such as love, romance, relationships, philosophy, humor, daily life, and God.

# 666: The THINGS HEREAFTER

**666: The THINGS HEREAFTER**     2009
ISBN:1441466479     LinAven Publications

*666: The THINGS HEREAFTER* is a Revelation Study Guide, complete with the AV text. Leaders of small study groups, Bible teachers, and preachers will find this an excellent aid in these 'last times.' In an outline form, it adapts itself well to all types of prophetical teaching. It will make an excellent addition to any library and a classic gift for any occasion.

Made in the USA
Charleston, SC
16 April 2010